Granite Creek Books

For Joseph —
May it all be as
full —

Joanne Fortin
H

JOANNE LINVILLE'S

SEVEN STEPS TO AN ACTING CRAFT

By Joanne Linville and John Deck

Joanne Linville's Seven Steps to an Acting Craft

Copyright © 2011 Joanne Linville and John Deck

Published by Granite Creek Books, Santa Cruz, CA, United States

ISBN 978-1-4507-5998-4

Quoted works:

W. Shakespeare, *William Shakespeare: the Complete Works*, S. Orgell, A Braunmiller, Eds.
New York: Penguin, 2002.

A. Chekhov, *Anton Chekhov Five Plays,* New York: Oxford, 1972.

Cover photograph: Ute Ville

Book design: Marc D'Estout

Printed at Watermark Press, San Francisco, California, USA

Contact: www.joannelinville.com

10 9 8 7 6 5 4 3 2 1

CONTENTS

Introduction

During the last class with Joanne she taught me something I'd never heard before from anyone I had studied acting with. She had told the students she wanted us to look at—to actually see—something that was imaginary. She wanted us to focus our eyes on the object so that we could describe it fully to others in the class. I had an idea right away and spent a few moments imagining that I was looking at an eagle perched on the top of a great pine tree.

When my turn came to describe my 'vision,' Joanne told the other students to watch me closely.

I saw their faces turn toward me, and, as they did so, the eagle began to fade away. I was able to describe what I had seen moments before. I tried to make the bird sound beautiful and noble, and searched my mind for descriptive terms that captured the color of the feathers and fierce, unblinking eyes. But what I was actually seeing was not the eagle, but the faces of the other students looking at me.

Joanne interrupted me in mid-description. She said she could tell that I had seen the bird moments before but wasn't seeing it at that moment.

I had to admit she was right. I asked her how she knew I wasn't seeing the imaginary eagle.

"Because I didn't see it," she said.

Tyler Lund, former student

The ultimate goal of Joanne Linville's acting classes is to find ways of making the audience believe in the actor. And not just for a single dramatic moment or for a single wonderful performance. Imaginary eagles have to be seen every time the lights dim and the curtains rise. Joanne calls upon virtually every aspect of a student's physical and mental being to achieve this single purpose. The demands her acting method makes on students are enormous and continuous. Success is cumulative, acquired over time in small increments through study, imagination, experimentation, physical and mental discipline and extensive practice. Her students have to be ready to make the sacrifices that total dedication to artistic excellence demands of the aspirant, the novice and the veteran actor alike.

Joanne has devised a seven-step method that lays out the foundation for the early development and continuous growth of the actor's craft. Much of the content of this book is taken up with naming and defining these steps. It is an introductory book, and in it the steps are introduced separately because a thoroughly developed and enduring craft requires mastery of each. In exercises, discussions and in performance the steps may combine and overlap.

Each step is essential to any person who wishes to gain the skills, self-confidence and adaptability that make great acting possible. Her technique provides the fundamentals for the beginner, and it reinforces and replenishes experienced actors who feel a need for renewal. Joanne feels strongly that acting classes are essential to the actor's growth and development. Seeing other students try, often fail, and sometimes brilliantly succeed in "getting it" is a critical part of the learning process.

The contents of the book are entirely based on Joanne's classes, her approach to acting and the teaching of acting. Her comments on student's work are quoted, paraphrased and summarized throughout.

STEP ONE

The Inner Life

Going to Your Inner Life

Seeing Inner Life on Stage

The Inner Life

One of the core demands of Joanne's method requires you to become familiar and comfortable with the way the human mind—yours included—works.

Like most humans, your thoughts are constantly shifting focus. One moment they are concentrating on what is going on immediately around you—as, at this moment, you are staring at type on a page, letting the letters form words, analyzing how the words arranged in a certain order become meaningful sentences. The next moment you may remember that you have an appointment to have your teeth cleaned at 2:30 this afternoon, and you wonder if there's enough money in your account to cover the check with which you intend to pay the hygienist. Thinking of the appointment ends your concentration on the book and transports you mentally forward in time to things that haven't happened yet—and that may not happen the way you think they will.

While you read this page you probably have a vague sense of the place where you're reading—the chair you're seated in, the light on the page, the air you breathe, the close and distant noises you hear. But all of that you can ignore completely—if this book contains information you are sure will be of great value to you in the future. You won't have to try to concentrate to keep your mind off the teeth cleaning.

This kind of reading without thinking is happening right now, as you see the letters N O W and put them together to form the word NOW. You spend a lot of time in the now, the immediate present, when you are working, conversing with people, buying a ticket, finding a seat in a movie theater. Human beings who save lives, write histories of western civilization or discover new planets, as well as those who pay the rent on time or parallel park their cars quickly in a very tight space, have to be concentrating on what they are doing right at the moment: working, meeting responsibilities or coordinating physical movement with what their eyes perceive of their surroundings. To succeed at even simple tasks, they must restrict their mental activity to the NOW moment.

In her classes, Joanne refers to this type of mental activity as living in the outer life, because the focus is on the surroundings, on actions that take place outside the self, on what is real around us.

There is another mental activity, another way of seeing and thinking, which Joanne refers to as the inner life. Many people spend more time living in the inner life than they do in the outer. They don't always find this a very flattering idea. It implies they aren't living in the real world where things happen that demand clear thinking. But it's true.

Joanne: *Suppose there may be one reader who is trying very hard to concentrate on the words printed on the page that you are reading right now. He is having difficulty concentrating on the printed words. His reading is interrupted by unwelcome thoughts like these:*

This room is way too hot. If someone doesn't turn the heat down, I'll get up and throw a chair through a window. I swear I will. Otherwise, I'll be asleep in two minutes.

Besides the heat, the glare of that overhead light blurs the print, makes it ten times harder to read. I should just go over and grab that reading lamp and bring it over here. No one's using it.

I have to move the lamp over here because the chair that it shines on is too comfortable. I sat on it once before and woke up an hour later without reading a single page.

When you want to concentrate, you'd better find a hard

*chair, without cushions. And no armrests. Like the chair
I'm sitting in now.*

*I have to finish reading this introduction. Right away. I
have to leave the house in half an hour. And before that,
wash up, change, be at the bus stop by four. It will take
me thirty minutes to get ready, so how much time do I
have? Where's my watch? Where'd I leave my watch?*

     Reading is an outer life activity. When we see
ourselves throwing chairs through windows and moving furniture instead of reading the page, when we worry
about catching busses and where we left our watches, we
have slipped into our inner life.

     In our inner lives we can do the impossible. May-
be that's why we spend so much time there. Miracles
regularly take place in our inner lives. The shyest person
can become the close personal friend of celebrities, the
envy of great artists, the person political leaders go to for
advice and someone linked romantically with the world's
most attractive people.

     This is not to say the inner life is the place where
you always get what you want. People can become ter-
rified of things they encounter in their inner lives, even
when there is nothing real threatening them. It's in their

outer lives that real dangers are more likely to lurk.

Sometimes circumstances force you to go into your inner life. There are classic situations when you escape into it. One such situation is when you are waiting for something to happen.

Joanne: *You are driving to work when a small accident occurs several blocks ahead. All the vehicles heading in both directions are stopped. You can't move. The traffic update on your car radio says that it will be at least 20 minutes before there is any change.*

What will you do for that time? Will you just sit behind the wheel and stare through the windshield, concentrating all your mental powers on watching one car up the line inch forward, so that all the cars between you and it will inch forward, so that, finally, you will get to inch forward? How much concentration does it take to keep an eye on a row of stopped vehicles?

One small part of your mental awareness is all that need be dedicated to a traffic jam. With the rest, you could imagine many things: You could worry about how your boss will act if you're late for a meeting. You might even imagine him raging at you in front of people you are competing with for a better job. You might see yourself patiently explaining that you left home in plenty of time, and that you didn't cause the problem, you weren't part of the accident.

Or you could make yourself furious once more about a new puppy that a new neighbor recently brought home to her apartment. It has barked all night every night since she got it. Should you call your landlord? The rental contracts say no pets allowed. Should you write her a pleasant note and sign it? Or a threatening one and not sign it?

Or you could spend the waiting time rehearsing the poem you are working on for your acting class. In your imagination you see yourself finishing the poem. Teacher and students are all silent. All stare at you with expressionless, pale faces. Then, after twenty seconds, they all begin to shout, jump around, wave their hands in the air. A deafening roar of applause fills the room.

The mind, when it is focused on the inner life, often dwells on things from the past, moving about through memories without trying to remember everything in detail. For instance, the person who thinks about his angry boss may have been late for meetings before. That would make it more likely that he will get into trouble. What if the person having the puppy problem has found the new neighbor attractive, dog or no dog, but doesn't want to admit it? How would that influence what he chooses to do?

The inner life often moves us into the future and suggests what might happen if we do something we haven't done yet. For example, the person who wants to get rid of the dog might think the following: "If I tell the landlord and she's evicted, I could never face her again even if I wanted to." All this anguish takes place in the imagination—the inner life—while in your outer life you are sitting in your car, waiting for the traffic to start moving again.

Going to Your Inner Life

In her classes, Joanne wants her students to become acutely aware of how their mental activity moves from outer life to inner life and back. She wants them to become comfortable with these changes and to think of them. She sometimes asks a student to go into his or her inner life—not wait until their inner life takes over because they are stuck waiting for something to happen. She has a very good reason for doing this.

If you are standing in front of a class with a poem or monologue to perform, and you are entirely in your outer life, you might be struck speechless by a flood of outer life distractions: wanting to succeed with the assignment, seeing teacher and students watching and listening, using words that may not be perfectly memorized and aren't part of your regular vocabulary. These are distractions that can cause paralyzing nervousness, dry mouth, weak voice, hands like lead weights hanging lifelessly at your sides.

That is an occasion when the ability to escape into your inner life can free you. When Joanne asks you to "go into your inner life," you have choices about where you will go and what you will find there. If you are presenting a poem or monologue from a play that is pleasant or romantic in nature, you might go right to memory, find an occasion when you were happy, when you were in pleasant surroundings or in a romantic frame of mind. You use the memory of images, sounds and feelings as a means of escaping the tension caused by the outer life's domination, which can interfere with your ability to concentrate on what it is you have to present.

In your inner life, you can borrow someone else's troubles and triumphs, especially if you have observed just how those troubles and triumphs were reflected in the person's behavior. You can think of things you have read or heard about from others. You can select from these possibilities whatever is needed to make the feelings that come out of the work your own. That is always the goal: to make the words and the feelings they arouse in you your own.

Joanne: *A person I knew was with an older woman, a friend, when she received news that her sister, who had been very ill, had died. The woman immediately began twisting a button on the sleeve of her blouse, looking only at the button. She asked questions while she twisted. When did she die? Where was she? Did she know what was happening to her? Was she in pain? She asked the questions while staring at and twisting this button. Her questions were very matter-of-fact and showed no emotion. They were outer life questions. Yet something else was going on in her mind. We don't know what. But I doubt very much if she was seeing the button she was looking at and twisting while asking about her sister's death.*

When an actor witnesses something like that, or just hears about it from others as I did, she collects the information, the images, the feelings. She stores them away and perhaps finds use for them later.

Seeing Inner Life on Stage

The inner lives of characters often supply highly dramatic moments in plays and on screen. In Shakespeare's tragedy, *Macbeth*, the title figure has been told by witches that he is going to become king. But there is already a king, Duncan, and the only way Macbeth can gain the throne is if Duncan dies. Macbeth, with his wife in total agreement, decides to kill Duncan. Alone and on his way to the king's bedchamber to commit the murder, he has an inner life experience that is unforgettable. He "sees" a dagger floating in the air before him. In a voice full of terror he says:

> *Is this a dagger that I see before me,*
> *The handle toward my hand? Come, let me clutch thee!*
> *I have thee not and yet I see thee still.*
> *Art thou not, fatal vision, sensible*
> *To feeling as to sight, or art thou but*
> *A dagger of the mind, a false creation*
> *Proceeding from the heat-oppressed brain?*

Macbeth is having the same kind of trouble keeping his mind on killing Duncan as the would-be reader was when the warmth and light of the reading room began to bother him. Of course, Macbeth's imagination, fed by ambition and the idea of murder, is on fire: he actually "sees" the murder weapon floating in the air in front of him. He reaches for it but can't touch it. And he knows that the floating dagger may be a creation of his mind, visible only in his inner life. He calls it a "dagger of the mind... Proceeding from the heat-oppressed brain." He's frightened of what he "sees," but he goes ahead with his plans anyway.

By the way, Joanne would insist that this "dagger of the mind" must be seen by the actor playing Macbeth, and seen so clearly that the audience sees Macbeth seeing it, like the imaginary eagle spoken of at the beginning of the book. More on focusing the eyes and the mind is covered in the next step.

Exploring how mental focus moves between inner and outer lives, getting used to the shifts, switching on purpose and using images, memories and feelings from the inner mind are fundamental skills, the foundation on which Joanne's acting system stands.

STEP TWO

Focus

An Aside: Actors Must be Fed

Focus

This book opened with an account of a student's breakthrough experience in one of Joanne's classes. The student failed to show her that he saw an imaginary eagle. Joanne knew he didn't see it because she could see that the student's eyes weren't focused on it. And when he understood what she meant, he had an epiphany—a moment of realization, understanding, and change.

But many of us have a question about this: How do you focus on something that isn't there? The short answer to that question: You put it there.

Through her years as an acting student, actress, director, teacher and an astutely critical member of many, many audiences, Joanne has observed that the actor's focus is the primary means of making the audience believe.

Joanne: *Whatever the actor is doing, seeing or thinking shows first in the eyes. To make the eagle perch in a treetop or a dagger float on the air for the audience, the actor has to see these things. They have to be real for him before they will be real to the audience. That means he has to create them in his inner life in detail—see the eagle blink its eyes, note the gold inlay in the dagger's handle. When you focus on the object, and the audience sees you seeing it, they know it's there.*

Joanne says that the eyes focus before the voice or gesture gives anything away. A suite of responses can follow that focus, anything from violent physical reaction to mental exertions that are masked by a perfect exterior calm. No matter where the the action is going on on stage, the eyes get there first.

In one of her classes, a student presented a monologue she had been rehearsing for weeks. Joanne was pleased with the performance generally.

Joanne: *You got the words right. You could put more feeling into the words, but there was something true about what you were doing. Because there was truth in your eyes.*

Just getting the words right, even if they are the words of William Shakespeare, George Bernard Shaw, Tennessee Williams or Harold Pinter, won't make them true. Not unless you believe them. And you have to show the audience that belief.

Focus shows the audience that you are caught up in the dramatic moment, that you aren't on a stage covered with scenery and crowded with actors, but in a place that your inner life has furnished with real things, even if imagined and remembered. The way you look at those things, and the way you respond to what you see, sends messages to the audience.

Imagine John Wayne in an old western, wearing a coonskin hat and deerskin shirt, on lookout. He's squinting into bright morning sunlight, looking for the enemy. The camera shows you when something changes in that squint: first the eyes open wider, just for an instant. Then they narrow again. The camera doesn't have to show us what he has seen. We know before he turns his head and shouts to his men, "Grab your rifles! Here they come!"

Eyes look inward as well as outward. While peering at what surrounds them, they can be blinded by images from the past brought to mind by something in the present, or by imaginary events that haven't taken place yet but could very easily happen in the future. In other words, the eyes can show when the mind changes focus, when some new thing grabs its full attention and what feelings the new object or individual inspires. When we are lost in private thoughts and a vivid, perhaps threatening, image from the outer world overshadows them, our eyes change. Our attention follows where our eyes take it. We change focus, even when we are gazing at imaginary, inner images and ideas, if another comes along and sweeps all away. Confrontations begin in the eyes, and the eyes tell us if negative feelings resulting from a disagreement are subsiding or continuing at full force.

The eyes can move from an unfocused inward look to a precise concentration on an object or person, and what they see may reverse what a person was thinking and feeling moments before. Suppose you dream of buying a ski cabin not far from Lake Tahoe if the prices of the stocks you own keep rising. Imagine yourself describing this cabin to a friend over the telephone. Where would your eyes be focused? Then, while speaking, you turn on the evening news and see that the stock market plunged today and that your stocks lost half their value. What happens when you try to focus on your imaginary ski cabin now? Does it look the same?

In one of Joanne's classes a student is asked to prepare a speech from *Romeo and Juliet.* In the play the two have just met and fallen in love. They want to be married right away. (This happened long ago, in Verona.) After the famous balcony scene, Romeo leaves Juliet to find the priest who will marry them. At nine o'clock the next morning, Juliet sends her nurse to meet Romeo and get the news about the wedding arrangements. Though Juliet's love for Romeo seems very mature, she is only thirteen, and she is impatient for Nurse's return, as a girl that age would likely be. She is alone on stage, waiting for Nurse to return.

> **Juliet:** *The clock struck nine when I did send the nurse;*
> *In half an hour she promised to return.*
> *Perchance she cannot meet him. That's not so.*
> *O, she is lame! Love's heralds should be thoughts,*
> *Which ten times faster glide than the sun's beams*
> *Driving back shadows over the lowering hills...*
> *Now is the sun upon the highmost hill*
> *Of this day's journey, and from nine till twelve*
> *Is three long hours; yet she is not come.*

It is essential that the actress have a sense of who and where she is physically and mentally so that she can communicate fully to the audience as Juliet. And this begins by focusing her attention on her surroundings as only Juliet can—as an impatient young woman waiting for information about the young man she loves and wants to marry.

She must see surrounding hills, among them the "highmost hill" where the noonday sun blazes down. She must see a road along which the Nurse will return. The road is empty. She doesn't see the carriage she is searching for, but she will be looking at all carriages that travel that road. She has been staring at the road for hours. With each carriage that comes into view she becomes hopeful. And she loses hope when it proves to be the wrong one.

> **Joanne:** *Before you speak, have your eyes focused on the hills beyond the town. Move a little closer to what you are looking at. Look over there, look over here, look wherever carriages can come from. When you don't see a carriage, how do you react? When you see the wrong one, how do you show it? Look again, look harder. Spot a carriage— over there. Is that it? Move closer, look again. No. It's the wrong carriage again. Now, when there are no carriages in sight, begin the monologue.*

> *"The clock struck nine when I did send the nurse."*

> *The action of the scene is the search. She doesn't give up, doesn't become frustrated. She is looking all the time she's speaking. You want to touch the audience with Juliet's excitement and eagerness to see what she is look- ing for and what she sees.*

On one occasion the student playing Juliet kept

the search going but didn't communicate the excitement
of a young woman in love.

Joanne: *Is that all the excitement Juliet feels? She
doesn't stand there like someone waiting for her grand-
mother's wagon to come home from the market. You
have to keep looking with all your might for the carriage
when you say those lines.*

*Give me the eyes of Juliet—what she sees out there where
news of Romeo will come from. She's seeing two things:
Romeo in her imagination, and the empty lane in reality
—what she wants to be there and what is really there.*

After a successful presentation of the same
material, Joanne sees real progress in the student's work.

Joanne: *Very good. You almost brought me to tears.
Your eyes were really out there, focusing on the empty
lane between two stone walls, sun on the stones. A
glaring sun. Your imagination started to make something happen. Your imagination—what you saw as
Juliet—was real for you and it became real to me. You
were Juliet for a second and it was all true for you. When
there is no focus, there's no truth.*

The importance of focusing cannot be overstated. Students get it for a moment and the moments add up. It is hard to keep because there are so many distractions. Not the least are the lines you have to say. But if you can focus your eyes as Juliet focuses hers, then it will be easier to make her lines yours. Joanne feels that the ability to become focused and to remain focused is a measure of your growth as an actor.

An Aside: Actors Must be Fed

A former student of Joanne's, Julie James, was playing the role of "Sylvia" in A. R. Gurney's play of the same name. Sylvia is a dog. Sylvia doesn't look like a dog and doesn't wear a dog costume. She even speaks English. But in mind and body, in all relationships with humans and other dogs, Sylvia is a dog.

Julie said of her role: "All the time I was preparing for the role, I kept asking myself: What feeds a dog?"

Joanne often speaks to her students of what is feeding the actor in a scene or monologue. Actors are fed by what gets and holds their attention, what demands their concentration, what forces them to respond, perhaps verbally, perhaps physically, but possibly by remaining still and seemingly passive. (Suppose someone points a gun at you and says: "Move and I shoot." The weapon "feeds" you an urge to run or dive for cover, but the warning feeds you the idea that diving for cover would probably be the wrong response.)

"Feeding" is a term that is used in sports, particularly basketball. You feed the ball—pass it or hand it—to a player driving for the basket. The player who is fed the ball takes it without breaking stride, jumps and lays the ball up for two points. When you are correctly fed, you score, but the feeding and being fed is a team effort. See *An Aside "Landing the Word"* (p.104) for more information about feeding.

What feeds the actor can be many things: What someone says or doesn't say, does or doesn't do; the stars in the sky; a familiar song coming from an open window of the apartment next to yours; the gun in the angry boy's hand; the emptiness of a room you lived in for four years when you are leaving it for the last time.

Joanne: *What feeds you may inspire, energize, frighten, confuse, drive mad, make happy, kill or bring back to life. You can be fed by the fear that the little cough you developed last night is the first sign of an incurable disease. You can be fed by the suspicion that someone who is engaged to a close friend has fallen madly in love* *with you. Either one of these sources of a "feed" will influence how you act. You can't make plans to travel in Europe next spring if this throat tickle is eventually going to kill you. You can't feel comfortable around someone who might at any moment beg you to run off with him or her, leaving your best friend in the lurch.*

Macbeth, when he sees the dagger floating in front of him, is "fed" by thoughts of the murder he is about to commit. Juliet is fed by her love of Romeo and her impatience with anything that keeps them apart.

Julie James' question is a good one to ask yourself before you begin to perform: What's feeding me in this monologue? What's feeding the character who says the lines I'll be repeating in class today?

Julie James, in the role of Sylvia, found the correct answer to her question about what feeds a dog, because people who saw her performance were convinced that she was indeed Sylvia, fed by the things that feed a dog like Sylvia. Hers was an excellent comic performance by a highly skilled actress.

STEP THREE

The Tenses

The Past Tense

The Present Tense

The Future Tense

More Verb Forms

The Tenses

Everyone who has ever had a class in English grammar remembers the three basic tenses: past, present and future. Tenses are used in spoken and written language to designate the time when an action takes place. I ran in the past; I run or I am running in the present. In the future, I shall run, I am going to run, I am running the marathon next week.

Tenses are important to an audience because they reveal where in time the mind of the speaker is focused from thought to thought, sentence to sentence. Our minds move around constantly, and that's true of people who aren't on stage as well as in written dialog.

Suppose you overhear something like this:

"I live here in Chicago now. I moved back in 2002. I should have stayed in L.A., stuck it out with the improv group I was working with. But I got this job in children's television. Now my friends have a theater in West Hollywood, and it's quite successful.

"And I'm here. I'm a green and purple zebra named Zippy in a pre-schoolers' TV puppet show four afternoons a week. My contract will be up in a couple of years. And when that happens, it'll be: 'See you later Zippy.'"

The speaker is in Chicago when he starts this complaint and is speaking in the present tense. He goes back to the past when he mentions what happened in 2002. "Now my friends have a theater," brings us back to the present. He remains in the present tense to talk about Zippy. When he starts talking about his contract, he moves into the future and his plans to leave the children's program.

Joanne: *What happened in the past, when he left L.A., is done with. He regrets it now, in the present, but he can't change that. What is happening now, in L.A., where his friends are enjoying success, and in Chicago, where he is only Zippy, isn't completed. It's open-ended. When something that is going on in the present is finally finished, it moves into the past.*

Finally, he speaks of the future where all sorts of things could happen. The improv group could break up. Or Zippy may be spun off, and he would get his own show— a full hour, five days a week on public television. Tenses guide the actor and audience through the time covered on the stage. Actors have to be aware of the tenses because each calls for a different attitude toward the situations being described.

The Past Tense

Because they are complete and took place previously, past actions are usually more vivid and less confusing to us than what is going on now. They are much more reliable than what we speculate might happen in the future. Of course, if you are involved in a dramatic event occurring in the present—if you are watching a building burn down, for example—what you are seeing will doubtlessly overshadow any fires you have seen previously, at least until it is put out.

But, as a rule, we are usually more comfortable speaking of the past because we have more facts assembled about what happened. The past has a beginning and an end. We can control what we describe or reveal about the past, decide which details to include and which we might want to leave out, and condense time so that we cover many years in a couple of sentences. We can adjust the past to suit the listener who might be confused as to the point of a story. Too few details can rob the story of suspense and lessen the excitement we are trying to convey. Too many may put the listener to sleep.

A lot of dialog has to do with the past. What do actors do, where do our eyes focus, when we are talking about the past? We may "see" what we are describing, but it isn't like a narrative unfolding on a movie screen.

In the first place, no one else can see it. If you are telling the story, you might have an unspoken reason for telling it. Maybe you want to make your listener feel the same emotions you felt when this event occurred or agree with a decision you made because of it. So you might glance at the listener's face, to see if what you are saying is having the impact you intend it to have.

> **Joanne:** *It's important to become aware of how you handle yourself physically and where your eyes focus when you speak about the past. Do they stare at a fixed object or person? Do they skim over the surroundings without stopping? If you want to be understood, if you want your listeners to agree with your point of view, you probably glance now and then directly at their faces to see how they are receiving the information. Note also that stories from the past can be relaxing and comforting. They can have frightening or humorous endings. The way the story ends is going to influence how it is told. Listen to how voices change in pitch and intensity depending on the content of what is being said.*

The Present Tense

We use the present tense to report on things and observe things that are going on right now, that are works and actions in progress, subject to change and incomplete:

"I'm hurrying to catch my flight."

"He's tired out. He wants to go to bed."

"A crowd has been gathering in the street—maybe forty people, maybe more. Some of them are carrying bricks and wooden clubs. And they're coming this way."

We don't know if the traveler got to the gate on time, if the person reached his bed before falling asleep, if the crowd passed by or stopped in front of the speaker. The present can generate excitement because it points the audience's attention toward the unknown, the possible, and keeps them guessing what will happen next. As soon as the action is complete, it belongs to the past.

When you are in the present tense, memory is usually on pause. Things are in motion and they take all your attention. Glancing at a wristwatch, concentrating on the names of streets you are passing from a bus window or looking for an old friend in a crowd are all present actions that create a kind of tension based on the need to know something, to find something out, to understand what is occurring around you so that you can act or respond.

What are the eyes doing when they are focused on the present? What are some physical behaviors you would associate with actions that are incomplete or ongoing, as opposed to things that are settled, over? Certain actions would seem to lock us into the present—driving a car, watching or participating in athletic events, trying on new clothes.

Joanne: *It was noted earlier that we often spend more time in our inner life than we do in our outer life. But the outer dominates when we are in the present tense. We focus on what we are doing, on what things are happening around us. Watch yourself and others when you are living in the present tense, the here and now. See if you can detect changes in physical expressions. Where are the eyes focused? Do they stare or seem to move about, as if searching for something?*

You have to be flexible when thinking of the tenses, because it is possible to see something in the present that takes you back into the past or forward into the future. The present situation may feed you a memory or a vision of what's to come.

The Future Tense

The past has happened and is based on fact. The present is happening, and we search it for facts in order to understand it. The future isn't so dependent on fact:

"I'm going to get the part. The way the director looked at me, I just know she'll call me this afternoon."

"We'll go to Alaska, get jobs in the cannery and make enough money to spend three months surfing in Puerto Escondido."

"This time I'll break off with Harry for good."

What you say about the future can be based upon your hopes, beliefs, determination, what you feel must happen if there is any justice, what has happened previously and should or should not happen again. What you say about the future isn't certain, but at the time you say it there's nothing to prove you're wrong. So how do you say it then? With absolute confidence? Or in a way that indicates you are pretty sure? Or are you trying to convince yourself that what you want to happen has to happen?

Could you watch and listen to someone say "This time I'll break off with Harry for good" and tell if that person is confident or still a bit unsure that the break-up will be final?

Once again the eyes have a way of showing us the truth. When we are uncertain of something, we have difficulty looking directly into the eyes of the person we are speaking to and maintaining that steady gaze. When we are sure, when we've made up our mind, our certainty comes with a steely, unwavering stare.

What happens to our voices when we are sure? Not so sure? Merely hopeful?

The future tense is often used to make bleak predictions. How do the eyes and voice handle an unpleasant and even threatening future?

"We'll never get our troops out of Afghanistan."

"She's strong. She'll pull through."

"Anyone who lives here will have to deal with a major earthquake within the next ten years."

Joanne: *Listen and watch people who are speaking of the future. Salesmen rely on it when they tell clients how happy, rich or beautiful their products will make them. But what about warnings of bad things to come, the people who predict disasters if we don't vote their ticket, send them contributions, join their group? Whatever their outlook, those who speak as if they know what the future will bring need confidence to add force to the facts they have at hand. The more outlandish their predictions, the more likely they will look you right in the eye and never admit there is any weakness in their argument.*

The following is an excerpted speech made by Doctor Astrov in Chekhov's play *Uncle Vanya*. The doctor, a man who is liked and respected by others, is not pleased with himself, his work or his entire existence. The first words he utters, "No, thank you," are spoken in the present tense. He is addressing an old nurse who has just offered him food. After he answers her, he speaks of the past and then, at the end of his speech, speculates on the future.

Astrov: ... *No, thank you... A few weeks before Easter I went to Malitskoye. They had an epidemic there. Typhus. There were village people lying around all over the place in their huts. Filth, stench, smoke everywhere and calves on the floor mixed up with the patients—little pigs as well. I was on the go all day—didn't so much as sit down or have a bite to eat. They brought someone in from the railway, a switchman. I got him on the table to operate and damned if he didn't die on me... Then, just at the worst possible moment, my feelings did come to life and I felt as guilty as if I'd murdered the man... I sat down and closed my eyes like this. And I thought of the men and women who will be alive in a hundred or a couple of hundred years after we've gone, those we are preparing the way for. Will they have a good word to say for us? You know, Nanny, they won't even remember us.*

The doctor describes past scenes of violent illness and death that would be painful, even unbearable, for most people to witness. He worked as hard as a man could, but in a fog of fatigue and hopelessness that dulled him to his task. There is no sense of accomplishment, and he is not making himself out to be a hero.

Joanne: *The doctor paces up and down, turning down the offer of food in the present tense, then going immediately and totally to the past, to memory, for what he wants to say. There is nothing in the play to indicate this change of tense between "No, thank you..." and "A few weeks before..." The actor would have communicated the change to the audience, looking first at the servant, then looking back, looking inward.*

He isn't giving us the full story of what happened in the past. It isn't a newspaper account. There are no dates, no numbers of those who became ill and of those who died. He includes strange details—like the animals lying sick among the stricken humans. It is personal, a memory, his own experience of the plague.

The main thing he recalls is an instance of failure, when he fails to save a man's life. His recollection lacks excitement and any feeling of pride, or even satisfaction, with his work. What people say about the past is often incomplete and can be misleading because they don't tell the whole story. His story may involve heroic effort, but that isn't what he recalls.

When the doctor speaks to Nanny again, he moves into the future, and wonders if people in centuries to come will know what happened in Malitskoye, and if they will have a positive word to say about what he did. He thinks not, but he can't possibly know.

He could be wrong. We in the audience admire Dr. Astrov for his modesty and selflessness and hope he is wrong.

It is important to note that Dr. Astrov's speech moves from past to present to future without any warning as to where his attention will settle next. He is being fed by images of the past and by questions and ideas about the future. This shifting in tenses occurs constantly in drama written in realistic language, and each shift denotes a change in the mental focus of the character. Actors have to be aware of these changes and change with them.

More Verb Forms

When the action takes place is not all there is to be said about tenses. Verb forms using auxiliaries—would, could, should, etc.—also refer to the time actions take place, but they add other elements to the meaning.

In the film *On the Waterfront*, Marlon Brando, at his best, plays the part of a former boxer, Terry Molloy, who early in his career threw a fight—lost it on purpose—because his brother and his backers told him to take a fall. In a single sentence that speaks revealingly of his career and life, Terry says: "I could've been a contender." He's saying he could have been one of the fighters who were in contention for the championship. He doesn't say he would have been champion. He doesn't even say he would have been the only contender—there were probably many. It does mean that all that is behind him, that he will never be anything again in the fight game. And all that information is conveyed by his saying, "I could have been." What he could have been is lost in Terry's past, but it still haunts him.

Common verb formations which we use all the time complicate the meanings of our speech. In acting, you enhance your performance when you are aware of these formations and how they affect meaning.

Step 4

Props

Props

At the opening curtain of *A Streetcar Named Desire*, the great Tennessee Williams play, Blanche Dubois appears on stage carrying a suitcase—the author calls it a "small valise." Joanne has seen the award-winning movie that was made of the play, as well as several stage productions, and in each case the actress playing Blanche, often a fine actress since it is a demanding role, failed to make the suitcase she carried real for the audience.

Joanne: *The actresses swung their suitcases around as if they were weightless—empty. Some dropped them or put them down as soon as they could and walked away from them, giving the audience the impression that there was nothing in the suitcase of any value to Blanche.*

But it isn't unimportant to Blanche. She doesn't have much of anything left in the world. She is poor, has lost the family home. By the way she handles the suitcase, Blanche can signal to the audience that whatever it holds is meaningful to her. How could she handle it so that the audience would know it contained something important? One thing she could do is set it down carefully, and not just anywhere. And if she walked away from it, perhaps she would turn and glance back at it. That's all it would take. The audience would see it and know something more about her—about who she is, how she feels coming to a city, penniless and in need of help.

The suitcase is a "prop," short for a stage property. There can be many props on view in drama and film. Every cup in a cupboard, every book in a bookcase is a prop. The cupboard and bookcase are props. The props Joanne asks her students to focus on in her classes are those that are handled, contemplated, discussed or pointedly ignored in a way that distinguishes them from other similar objects.

Joanne wants her students to "experience" the props they use. If the actresses playing Blanche Dubois had fully experienced their suitcases, each would know how much it weighs and that it contains clothing that may once have been fine but is now worn, inexpensive costume jewelry and cosmetics to conceal Blanche's fading beauty. These things, in combination with her threadbare charm and the soft lighting that will hide her flaws, she hopes will make a favorable impression on the people she meets in New Orleans, particularly men, one of whom may help her escape her past. Blanche's suitcase, fully experienced, contains her past failures and hopes for her future.

In Joanne's classes you begin working with props that you create in your imagination. You alone can see them to begin with. You give them dimensions, shape, weight. How you lift them and what muscles are required in the effort tell the audience if they are heavy or light. If they are fragile or precious, you show it by the way you pick them up, move them, set them down.

Joanne: *Once you have experienced props that you create in your imagination, using real props on stage will be much easier for you and more effective for the audience. Even though props are inanimate, you give them life as it unfolds in the play. I can't overemphasize how valuable props can be to the actor. There are times when the way the actor handles a prop tells the audience more about what is going on than the words the actor speaks.*

As a class exercise in experiencing props, students are asked to approach the door of their imaginary dwelling place—be it a home, cabin, apartment or motel room—carrying an imaginary bag of groceries. They are asked to take an imaginary door key out of their imaginary pockets or purses, open the door, step into a kitchen, set the bag on a table and begin removing items from it.

This sounds like a pretty straightforward task, but the description above doesn't contain enough information for the student to experience the props—bag, key, door, table, items in bag—involved in the scene.

For one thing, you would have to know what's in the bag you are carrying. You would have to fill it with items that are also imaginary but that you can experience. Here, as examples, are three bags full:

Bag one contents: seven frozen TV dinners—a week's supply of evening meals for the person carrying it.
Bag two contents: an expensive filet mignon, an expensive piece of cheese, potatoes, expensive salad greens and dessert and a very expensive bottle of wine.
Bag three contents: a ten-pound bag of dry cat food, a five pound bag of kitty litter, eight cans of cat food and a toy mouse that squeaks when pounced upon by a cat.

Suppose all three bag carriers have a few things in common. They stopped by the same store on a Friday night after a long week of work to make their purchases. All are tired. Each lives alone, except for the cat owner.

Joanne: *This is an exercise in mime, in which the actor has to communicate everything by movement and* *gesture and expression. It all must be planned out in advance, and every movement has to add to the creation of the character, his or her situation and feelings.*

By the way you carry your bags, I want to see that one bag weighs about twenty pounds, one contains a bottle of expensive wine, and one person doesn't care too much what he eats for supper. How can you show me that? Do you use two arms to hold the heavy bag? Do you wrap your arm around the one with the wine and press it against your chest? How carefully do you hold the bag containing the TV dinners?

Getting a key out of a purse or pocket when you are carrying something can be tricky if the burden is heavy or contains items that are fragile. Would you set the bags down on the front step before reaching for your key? Would you set them down the same way? If the heavy bag falls over, the cans of cat food may roll out, but that wouldn't mean much. But if the wine bottle fell, that could be trouble. Show me the difference in the way you set the bags down.

How would the TV dinner eater get out his key?

Do you unlock and open the door with the bag in your arms? Or do you wait until the door is open before picking it up? Does having a pet waiting inside the door influence the way you open the door? What is another way the pet owner could let the audience know there is a beloved animal inside?

What do they do with the keys when the door is open? Once inside, each person should unpack in a different manner. How might the groceries be taken out of the bag that would show the audience an important meal will be made from them this very night? How might the pet owner show feelings for the pet by the way the items are unpacked?

What could be done with the TV dinners to show that eating supper is not of major interest to the person who purchased them?

This is not to say that every possible way of experiencing a prop has to be shown. Drama is rarely centered on a single prop. More often, props indirectly contribute to the dramatic tension. But props, when fully experienced, show the audience something about the person who is working with them. They contribute to the identity that takes form from language, action and situation. Earlier we discussed the idea of an actor being fed by a person, a thing or an idea on stage. The grocery bags in this exercise feed the student. They can hint at a lonely existence, at the company a pet provides that offsets such loneliness, at the hope that a fancy meal with a friend might provide a way out of loneliness. Props can reveal something to the audience that the person handling them doesn't know.

Here is another exercise from one of Joanne's classes. A student has been given the assignment of writing with a quill pen. Again, the pen, paper, desk and whatever is being written are all imaginary. Again, she suggests ways of exploring the props that will allow them to be experienced.

Joanne: *Show me right away that you are not picking up a ballpoint pen. Ballpoints are stubby little things. They don't drip. They contain ink so you never have to think about keeping the tips supplied with ink.*

If you don't know how quill pens work, go to your library and look in art books for paintings and illustrations from before the 20th century. And find movies and television programs from that period. There are plenty of quill pens used in Masterpiece Theater Classics.

Using a quill involves using related props. You need an inkwell where you dip the pen and wipe off excessive ink. You also need a blotter to lift extra ink off the paper before it dries. You need a stand or pen-holder where you can leave the pen when you are pausing to reread what you have written. You need paper, of course. Paper was more precious in the days of quill pens. People didn't waste it, didn't start scribbling away, confident that they could wad up and throw out their mistakes.

What about light? You probably would use a candle in the quill pen era. You'd light the candle, but how? And you would place it where it would illuminate the page.

When quills were used, not as many people could read or write. Penmanship, a lost art in our time, was regarded as a sign of education and refinement. So you would be careful, you would write with a certain flourish, and you might go back over your writing to admire it, and to darken a dot over an i or add a comma.

You think before you write and pause while you are writing to plan your next sentence. Maybe you brush your face lightly with the feathered tip of the pen while you are thinking. Maybe you quit when the feather tickles your nose.

When you finish, blot your page, put your pen away, wiping
off the tip. Read what you have written carefully, take up
the pen again, dip it in the inkwell, and sign with a flourish,
because signatures in those days were more than just names,
they were identifiers, like personal stamps.

Props contribute to the actor's ability to convince the audience that what they are witnessing is real. When there is nothing false or forced in the way the prop is used, the audience has to believe what they are seeing, even if they are not familiar with what is taking place on stage—writing with a quill pen, for example.

Joanne: *When you fully experience your props, you own them. Once you own them, they never change. They will always be there for you. They can help you, they can guide you. Sometimes they seem almost to speak to you, giving you reassurances that what you are doing is right and true.*

STEP FIVE

Place

Making Your Place on Stage

A Broader Definition of Place

Filling in Your Place

Nora's Place in "A Doll's House"

Alone at a Garden Party

Place

When Joanne studied acting with Stella Adler, students didn't work with spoken language for the first full year. Acting was movement without words, but it encompassed a variety of physical expressions that exhibited conflict, character development, interaction of characters and the communication of a broad range of emotions.

One point of this year of silence was to give fitting emphasis to the physical nature of performance. Physical expression is the fundamental aspect of acting. All acting begins with it. Even without language an audience can see and feel the impact of large dramatic gestures—scenes of battle, the respect the people pay to emperors and heroes, the cunning and connivance of villains, the buffoonery of clowns. Action is communicated in small movements as well; sometimes changing the focus of your eyes and shifting your attention conveys a major shift in the flow of action.

To allow your physical self to communicate ideas and feelings fully, you have to be very comfortable and free—you could almost say "at home"— wherever you are performing. One of the seven steps in Joanne's technique is devoted to helping you become accustomed to being on stage by finding and experiencing what Joanne calls "place."

Making Your Place on Stage

In an exercise, Joanne asks students to step into an open area—whether it is an empty stage or an open space in the classroom. She will suggest that a chair or two be left in the cleared area. These chairs will represent the furniture you will use in a room she wants you to recreate for yourself and create for the people who are watching you.

> **Joanne:** *Imagination and memory are all you need for this exercise because you've been in this place before. I want you to recreate a familiar place so that we can see it. It could be your bedroom at home, an apartment you once shared with a roommate, the place where you are living now. So go into your inner life and use what you find there to make it real.*

> *Start by surrounding yourself with walls, ceiling, and floor. You have to see them; you have to give the place shape and dimensions. Let in light—from a window, from a lamp. Give it a smell—of coffee, of a candle, of the fumes from the street outside.*

> *Furnish it with things you know. The chairs you left in the space now have to be transformed into familiar*

furniture of your remembered room—your favorite
chair for reading, a couch you used for day-dreaming.

Continue to work on the room in your imagination. Is there
a rug on the floor? What about pictures on the walls, papers
and books on shelves and tables? What are the pictures of?
Are the papers and books neatly stacked or scattered? These
are things only you can see, but they are what will make the
room yours. A familiar room is full of familiar things.

Right now, while you are creating the place, you are
standing outside, putting it all together. Now it is time
for you to enter the room.

We haven't discussed what time it is. Make it night, late.
You've just come home. You open the imaginary door
and the room is now dark. You know where the closest
light switch is. Find it. Turn the light on.

What you see and feel is home, a pleasant welcoming
place where you belong. Let this place feed you a feeling of
familiarity and safety. If you are carrying something, put
it down on a coffee table. But you have to see the coffee
table before you put anything down on it. Otherwise we
in the audience won't know what you are doing.

Feel the air. Is the room warm or cold? If it's cold, you might turn on the furnace. If it's warm, you might open a window. Do you turn on the television or radio? Do you check your messages?

Actions of this sort have to be performed with absolute certainty. You know where the switches are. You know what furniture you have to step around in order to reach the window. Snap the necessary switches, turn the dials. Then go to a chair and drop into it as if exhausted.

Make yourself comfortable. Relax enough so that you begin to feel tired. Show us how relaxed you are—kick off your shoes, loosen your clothes, yawn noisily.

Of course, sitting or sprawling in your familiar room is not dramatic. There is no tension, no threat. But there could be. And the tension and threat will be all the more intense, exciting and disturbing to an audience if you are truly, convincingly in the place you have created and are experiencing the comfort and safety it affords you.

Joanne: *Now, just as you are getting drowsy, something strange happens that changes your place. The electrical power fails. The lights go out. The music or the voices on the answering machine are silenced.*

Only you know it. We in the audience will only know what has changed about your place by watching what you do, how you react.

So what do you do when it gets suddenly dark and silent? You have to show us what has happened and what that means to you.

Do you quickly get up off your chair or couch? How will you show us you can't see? Do you go back to the light switch you used earlier? If you do, how will your movements change? How well do you navigate in the dark? Where exactly is that coffee table relative to the chair you were sprawled in? Do you bump into it? Do you reach for it, and for other objects that you don't want to hit or knock over? Do you have to feel your way through the place you know so well?

When you determine that power is indeed shut off, what do you do next? Let's say you have a flashlight or candles and matches stored away across the room from you.

Begin to move across the remembered room in the dark. Again, there are hazards, things you might bump into, things to knock over. Walk into something. Hit your shin on a sharp edge. Do you shout, cry, become furious when you hit something in your own room?

Finally you reach the desk drawer, or the cupboard drawer or shelf, where the flashlight is. Open it, reach in, feel around for the flashlight. Get it in your hand.

Try it.

What do you do now, when the flashlight doesn't work?

Many scenes in horror movies begin with someone feeling perfectly safe and at home in a familiar place when the lights go out and something begins scratching at the windows or pounding on the door. The more the actor in that scene experiences that friendly, welcoming place initially, the more frightening the claw-like hand will be when it smashes through the door panel, grasps the doorknob and pulls the door out of the doorframe.

A Broader Definition of Place

Place can encompass much beside physical location and time of day. The season, calendar year, historical era, geographical location, nationality, family position, social class, political situation can all contribute to the sense of place.

The Diary of Anne Frank presents an extreme example of how experiencing place carries a drama forward. Families of Jews have been hidden in an Amsterdam attic from the Nazis who patrol the streets below, looking for Jews who are illegally concealed, like Anne's family is. If they are found, they will be transported to concentration camps where they will be exterminated.

Each of the characters in the play experiences the place differently, depending on many factors. Anne is young, intelligent and imaginative. She's seen looking out of small windows at the sky, welcoming the little daylight that barely penetrates the attic. Others don't experience that light and air as she does. She and a boy who is also hiding in the crowded attic fall in love under circumstances that would seemingly prohibit such feelings from ever developing. The adults have lost everything and feel trapped and hopeless. Anne, sharing the same place with them, escapes the confinement and hopelessness by way of her imagination and affection.

So the place experienced won't be exactly the same for everyone occupying it, even when the same forces—historical, social, educational, political, national, ethnic, etc.—act upon each of them. The more you know about these forces that influence the play, the easier it will be to imagine yourself living in your place, and that will aid in your performance.

Filling in Your Place

It's not easy experiencing place in Shakespeare if you haven't any inkling of what living was like when and where the drama is located. The plays take place in different countries and in different historical eras. There are filmed and otherwise recorded performances of Shakespeare's plays by a range of actors and acting companies. There are illustrations for some of the printed plays. Learning all you can about the time and place of the play, becoming familiar with costumes and customs, as well as familiarizing yourself with the full cast of characters and the action, will also help you feel confident in your place.

You will still have to go into your inner life, open up your imagination to the Shakespearian past and adapt your personal experiences and observations to the setting and conditions of the drama. You'll still have to focus your eyes and your attention on real and imaginary objects and people. You will have to give the props that you and others use the right weight, size and meaning.

Nora's Place in *A Doll's House*

In one of Joanne's advanced classes a student was working on the opening scene of Henrik Ibsen's *A Doll's House*. Nora, the main character, a middle-class housewife, has just come in from shopping for Christmas and her arms are full of parcels. Behind her a porter carries in a Christmas tree she purchased. Nora's actions in the scene are simple enough: She comes into the room humming a tune, puts her parcels on a table, tells her maid to hide the tree from the children and asks the porter how much she owes him. When he asks for sixpence, she gives him a shilling and tells him to keep the change. And she takes a macaroon from her pocket, nibbles it, puts it back.

The student assigned the part of Nora successfully repeats the few lines Nora has and completes the actions, but Joanne wants her to do more.

Joanne: *Sorry, but you are definitely not in Nora's drawing room. You are not in Norway in the late 1800s. And it doesn't feel like Christmas in a cold country. You are on stage right here, on Hollywood Boulevard, in this classroom. Your focus is good. You seem to be carrying* *packages. You do what has to be done. But it's all in your head. The rest of your body isn't here yet.*

Ibsen's play created a kind of scandal when it was first produced because Nora discovers that she is treated not as a human but as a sort of doll living in a doll's house. The play takes place at the end of the 19th century. Her husband is a banker. Her society is traditionally male-dominated, and as a woman she is relegated to a lesser role in family and societal affairs.

Her home seems modest but very comfortable, but something is wrong. She is treated like a child and not allowed to make decisions on her own. She has broken a rule, borrowed some money to give to someone in need without asking her husband for permission. Her husband—for that matter, everyone she knows—would disapprove of a housewife's borrowing money without the husband's guidance. Only men can be trusted to handle money.

Joanne: *Of course you can't fully develop Nora in the opening scene. But you can hint at something being wrong in that comfortable house right from the start just by the way you have her experience her place there. Suppose Nora, who lives in this doll's house, can't make up* *her mind where to put down the parcels. First she puts them on the table, then picks them up as if to move them again, starts to hand them to her maid, then puts them back on the table.*

Nora tips the porter more than is expected. Maybe she takes one coin out of her purse, puts it back, and takes a bigger coin out, pretending that the money means nothing to her. She could also hide the macaroon, nibble at it out of sight of the others because even buying sweets might be considered an extravagance.

These small gestures have to flow naturally as she bustles about. They can't be exaggerated. But they tip the audience off—send the message that this woman isn't sure of herself, even in her own home, right from the start.

And when, a few moments later, her husband, who is offstage, calls her his "little lark" and his "little squirrel," these childish names will resonate with her flighty and uncertain actions. Pet animals are kept in cages. The place Nora experiences at the end of the play is like a cage, and, in order to save herself, she has to escape it.

Alone at a Garden Party

Another of Joanne's classroom exercises involves an imaginary garden party where a guest—you—arrives and doesn't recognize anyone in the crowd. The actions are simple, but they depend for effect on the imaginative use of a prop, a glass of champagne. There are many different ways of handling this glass that will fill in the surroundings and communicate to an audience a sense of the party and of the guest's experience of place.

The exercise can be broken down into individual actions: The guest gets a glass of champagne from one of the trays brought around by waiters, takes a couple of sips, waves to someone who looks familiar but who doesn't respond. The guest takes a swallow of the champagne, then empties the glass. The guest puts the empty glass on a passing waiter's tray. But when another waiter comes by carrying full glasses, the guest gets another glass.

Joanne: *If you are alone at a party, you might need a drink to keep you company. But you may be shy about stopping a waiter carrying a tray of champagne glasses. Suppose several waiters pass by and none stops long enough for you to take a glass. You watch them pass. You smile and tentatively reach out, trying and failing* to get the waiter to offer you a glass. Finally you have to stop a waiter to get one.

Champagne comes in a stemmed glass. How do you take hold of the stem? Which fingers hold it? What if your glass is filled to the brim? How do you handle it when you take it off the tray? Does any spill? How do you react if a few drops spill on your clothing? Do you have a napkin to dab at it? Holding the palm of your free hand under the glass while you drink from it will keep any more from spilling, but it looks a bit awkward.

Now, with a glass in your hand, look around. If you are surrounded by strangers, most of whom are drinking champagne also, you might lift your glass and display a half-smile to show others that you are friendly and open to conversation. But if no one responds after a few such lifts, what happens to the smile?

Champagne tastes like a celebration. It brightens your mood. How can you show how much you like it? One easy way would be to follow your first small sip with a quick, bigger, second one—a gulp. You take it because the wine tastes so good. But maybe you embarrass yourself slightly by taking the second swallow. Until you think to yourself: Who cares?

Drink more. Begin to relax. Hear for the first time the music. How do you show that you like the band and the selections?

Now see someone you think you know, over there through the crowd. But you aren't sure it's who you think it is. Move around to get a better view. You might even bump into others while you are looking. You apologize with a smile, a nod, a shrug. Finally, you are sure. So you wave.

But the person doesn't see you, or doesn't recognize you, or, worse, doesn't want to recognize you. What happens to your champagne mood now? This is when you take not a sip, but a big swallow. And another.

Oh, look, you've emptied your glass. How embarrassing! You place it on a passing tray. But you look around and see that no one has noticed your behavior, that no one cares what you do.

And suddenly your champagne mood returns. When you see a waiter with a tray of full glasses, move toward him. Tap him on the shoulder. When he turns, take another glass.

And give the waiter a big smile of gratitude. He's your
best and only friend at the party.

As an actor, your place in a performance may
be in the middle of a vast desert in the time of the Pha-
raohs, in a cramped elevator stuck between floors after an
earthquake, on a rocket ship hurdling through space in
the year 3000 or in the lobby of a fleabag hotel in Newark
in 1930. Whatever the location, you have to find ways of
experiencing the place, making it yours and yours alone,
in order to belong there for the sake of the other actors
and the audience.

STEP SIX

Breathing

How Do Great Lovers Breathe?

Breathing

This is a simple step. Breathing is something we all do all the time without giving it any thought—if our health is good. We all know something about how we breathe—fast when running, slow when sleeping. We know that such changes in the rhythm and depth of our breaths are normal. We know why we breathe. We need to inhale oxygen and exhale carbon dioxide to live. We don't ordinarily think about the act of breathing any more than we think about keeping our hearts going.

Joanne: *Actors have to work on their breathing because people breathe in response to more than just the physical demands of existence. Often what you see, think and feel influences your breathing.*

Suppose you see someone who is arguing over a cell phone just as he is about to step off the curb into heavy traffic. Before you shout, "Stop!" or "Look out!" you will inhale quickly, so quickly you probably won't notice it.

Now, imagine yourself finishing the last question of the hardest final exam you have ever taken in your school career. You might exhale to mark the conclusion with a loud sigh that anyone listening would interpret as meaning: Thank God that's over.

Or you hear a strange scraping noise at your bedroom window at night. You have just moved into a neighborhood where homes have been burglarized. That scraping sound speeds up your breathing. You inhale often, deeply, in silence, as if storing oxygen away for a possible emergency exit.

Then you get up, look out the window, and see that the wind is blowing a branch of a rose bush against the glass. You exhale explosively and that breath comes out of feelings of shame and disgust: You were frightened by nothing.

We breathe before we speak or act. We breathe one way when we are angry, another when we're proud, another when we're worried. We breathe in a way that gives a hint of what we are thinking, even what we are about to do or say in response to what is feeding us at the time.

Earlier we discussed how important focusing the eyes is in acting. Only if the actor sees the object will the audience believe the object exists. But when the actor sees, one indication of his seeing is communicated by the change in breathing. People in the audience breathe the same way people on stage should breathe. A sigh or a gasp can function like a statement in a very primitive language that everyone speaks and understands.

Sigh = bored, tired, fed up, hopeless.

Gasp = surprise, upset, anger, fear.

How Do Great Lovers Breathe?

When Romeo and Juliet first meet, they are at a banquet. Romeo, a member of the Montague family, is crashing the party, wearing a mask. The party is being given by his family's most hated enemies, the Capulets. Juliet is a Capulet. The two young people meet as strangers, are immediately attracted to one another, but soon must part, kissing "by the book" of etiquette—that is, with respect rather than the tenderness or passion they feel. But however calm the kiss seems, both are in love.

Juliet's nurse tells her that her mother wishes to see her, and she obediently leaves. Romeo can't take his eyes off her. He speaks to Juliet's nurse.

Romeo: *What is her mother?*

Nurse: *Marry, bachelor,*

Her mother is the lady of the house,
And a good lady, and a wise and virtuous...
Romeo: *Is she a Capulet?*
Oh dear account! My life is my foe's debt.

How do you suppose Romeo is breathing when he watches Juliet leave? How when he turns and speaks to Nurse?

What happens to his breathing when he discovers that she is a Capulet?

Juliet is equally taken by Romeo. She wants to know who he is. (Both she and Romeo ask: What is she? What is he? They mean, of what family is she or he a member?) She asks her nurse to find out.

Juliet: *What's he that follows there, that would not dance?*
Nurse: *I know not.*
Juliet: *Go ask his name?—If he be married,*
My grave is like to be my wedding bed.
Nurse: *His name is Romeo, and a Montague,*
The only son of your great enemy.
Juliet: *My only love, sprung from my only hate!*
Too early seen unknown, and known too late!

Joanne: *The actress playing Juliet begins, "What's he that follows there," breathing her excitement and enchantment. Before she speaks, she inhales sharply and then says: "If he be married..."*

Breathing communicates her feelings of love, delight and fear to the audience before she uses words to express those feelings, almost before she herself knows what those feelings are.

Even if members of the audience have trouble with Shakespeare's Elizabethan English, they get a sense of the thoughts, and the emotions engendered by those thoughts, through the breath—if the actor is so much into his inner life that he goes there even for the air he breathes.

There is much more about breathing that has to be considered. This introduction is restricted to inhaling. Joanne gives exhaling equal attention in her classes. She also teaches restraint. Breathing on stage has to appear natural, unrehearsed. It shouldn't call attention to itself. It doesn't telegraph the story. It adds to it.

STEP SEVEN

Experiencing the Word

First, Lose the Meaning

Experiencing Poetry as an Actor

Experiencing Words on Stage

An Aside: Landing the Word

Experiencing the Word

Joanne: *There's a story about the great American actor, John Barrymore. I read it somewhere, and I've repeated it many times, probably expanded on it, changed it, because it helps students understand what I mean by "experiencing the word."*

Barrymore goes to an acting coach who sits him down in a comfortable chair next to a table on which there is a red apple in a small white dish.

"Mr. Barrymore, what do you see in that white dish on the table to your right?" the coach asks.

Barrymore glances at the plate, shrugs and says, "An apple."

"Mr. Barrymore," the coach asked again, "what do you see in that white dish on the table?"

"That?" says Barrymore, in his majestic baritone voice. "That object in that plate is a red apple."

And again, "Mr. Barrymore, what do you see in that white dish on the table?"

"Apple," snaps Barrymore, without looking at the table.

"Mr. Barrymore," the coach says, and repeats herself.

She asks him the same question again and again.
And he tries to answer in a way that will satisfy her.
He makes his apple sound happy, sad, important; he
makes it as bright as the apple of someone's eye and as
serious as the apple on William Tell's son's head. After
each attempt the coach asks him the same question.

Finally, the great Barrymore is exhausted.

And still the coach persists. "Mr. Barrymore, what do
you see in that white dish on the table?"

Barrymore stares long and hard at the apple in the plate.
It isn't the apple he saw when she first asked the question.
It is now a mystery. It is Adam and Eve's apple from the
Tree of Knowledge, and the apple in mom's apple pie, and
the one that keeps the doctor away. It is the sound of someone biting an apple, the work of chewing, the sweetness of
the juice, the act of swallowing, the taking of the next bite.
And, at the same time, it is less. It is just a word, the name
of a common fruit, the sound of two syllables.

"Apple," Barrymore hears himself say, the word coming up out of his depths, not with the puny definition he had given it previously. It is much larger, more complex and important. It is as if the apple is defining itself, speaking through him, using his voice to establish its identity to humans for the first time.

Apple.

Finally, having heard what she had wanted to hear, the coach moves on to the next exercise. For there is always more to be learned, even by a great actor.

We don't know how Barrymore said apple, but we can guess that he put a different feeling and gave a different sound to the word each time he repeated it then, and maybe for the rest of his life. The coach forced him to examine it in a way most people would have no reason to look at the word. She clearly didn't doubt that he understood its meaning, that he had grasped its definition. That was evident from the start. But when he sorted through the many usages of the word apple that make it more than just a fruit, as in the Adam and Eve story, when eating the apple against God's command meant expulsion from the Garden of Eden, she was reminding him that the word's meaning had extensions that connect to ideas and events that don't grow on trees.

Whatever the coach wanted from Barrymore, and her objective isn't absolutely clear, she was showing him that as an actor interested in improving his performance—and why else would he be seeing an acting coach?—he should be aware of all those meanings so that, when it is spoken in drama, the word will communicate the exact meaning that is intended from among all the meanings that could be attached to it. It has to work for the person who is speaking and for the speech or poem in which it appears.

The last of the seven steps, "Experiencing the Word," is about getting to the meaning of words and using them the way they are meant to be used—by the actor.

Joanne: *We have all kinds of personal experiences with words. We start playing with sounds when we're infants. Words could make us laugh or cry before we could speak them.*

Besides the meanings we learn from others and from books, we have images and ideas associated with words stored in memory. When we read or hear or speak words like hero, anger, love, terror, embarrassment or pain our minds recall images of actions, of people, of real and imaginary situations that we associate with heroics, attraction, shame and suffering. Other people, using those same words, have their own images and ideas. Our language belongs to everyone, but each of us adds something to the meaning of words that is ours alone.

We can be fairly comfortable and confident using words like hero, anger, love, courage, fear, death, survivor in our normal speech because the images and ideas associated with those words are not far from our personal experience. But actors are not playing themselves on stage. The spoken language they use is often written in a style that bears little resemblance to their normal language. The vocabulary and sentence structure can be old fashioned and, to people not used to them, awkward and unnatural. Sometimes speeches sound like poetry and even look like poetry on the printed page. But if they are read as poetry, with pauses after every line and accents to emphasize the meter, they may make very little sense to the actor or to the audience.

Joanne: *I use Shakespeare, Walt Whitman and T.S. Eliot when working on experiencing the word. Shakespeare was the greatest dramatist to write in English*

and probably in any other language. He was as well a
great poet. He has been dead for four hundred years.
Walt Whitman, whose poetry was meant to speak for
all the people of the United States of America in a voice
that was as fresh and original as the nation itself, lived
in the 19th century. Eliot was born in America but
became a citizen of England. He won the Nobel Prize
for Literature in 1948.

The words of these great men—coming out of the very
distant, quite distant, somewhat distant past—can be
terrifying to students. Just the names of the writers can be
intimidating. I don't mean because students can't under-
stand the meanings. The problem is more personal than
that. Students sometimes wonder how they could dare,
here in the early part of the 21st century, to speak the
words of Shakespeare and Whitman—and speak them
in public, to an audience that may include people who
love these very words and worship these masterful writers.

Joanne believes that when the language of the
assignment frightens or intimidates you, the audience will
hear it. Even if you have memorized the lines perfectly,
the audience will know that the words aren't yours. They
come to hear the truth. They want to believe the words
you are saying. They want to believe you.

First, Lose the Meaning

Her training in experiencing the word begins with a simple idea. Turn the words over and empty them out—get rid of dictionary definitions and personal definitions. Forget about the four hundred years since Shakespeare, forget how different the United States was when Whitman described it, forget Eliot's Nobel Prize.

She admits that emptying words of all meaning is an impossible task, but she wants you to try. She wants you to start with the basic stuff. Go back to the sounds. Play with them like you did as an infant. Say "round" so it sounds round. Fool around with words. Can you make square sound as square as round sounds round?

Is quick faster than fast? Is fast faster than swift?

Does moon sound more like a moon than sun sounds like a sun?

Must a tall man be large? Must a short man be small?

Must a large boy be tall? Must a small boy be short?

Joanne: *Suppose you do as instructed, turn a group of words over and empty them of meaning, words like thin, thrilling, flat, zigzag, calm, spike, boring, cantankerous. You try to get rid of their meanings, but as soon as you*

hear or read them, you know what they mean. You've
heard them all your life. A lot of them sound like what
they mean—like calm, thin, flat, light. Cantankerous
isn't so common, but it sounds like a quarrel. It is an irritating word, and quarrelsome and irritating are descriptive terms that appear in the definition of cantankerous.

Beside broad definitions, you have those images
and memories and other associations that are attached to
the words. You even have little sayings that go with some
of them: thin as a dime, light as a feather, flat as a pan-
cake, calm as a lake.

Zigzag, with its two z's and two syllables, looks
and sounds like what it means.

Two of the words, thrilling and boring, sound a
bit alike. If you read them in a list of similar words, like
tiring, thrilling, straining, soaring, sighing, boring and
soothing, none of them would necessarily fill your mind
with images and ideas. But taken individually, they would.
And these associations are so strong they make you feel
like an authority on experiences you've never had. You
don't have to have been ill to know that a slow recovery
from a serious illness can be boring. You don't have to be
a mountain climber to know it would be thrilling to reach
the summit of Mount Everest.

Joanne: *I once spent a complete class working on the first six words of the most famous speech in a play filled with famous speeches, the first words of Hamlet's soliloquy:* To be or not to be. *It was probably punishing for the students, but several of them were working on Shakespeare, and they were struggling with him—with his language and meaning.*

In their voices, there was something so unnatural, so lacking in confidence, that I could almost hear their thoughts: "Oh, God, Shakespeare again. And Hamlet, *no less. Full of poetry. Written in Elizabethan English. What am I doing here?"*

They knew what the six words meant. The idea is pretty simple, at least on the surface. In the full speech, Hamlet is thinking through the pros and cons of committing suicide. But the play is classical, it's historical, it takes place in Denmark and the playwright is the best ever, so his speeches are weighted down, the simple words feel heavy, and they can leave the student tongue-tied.

So I told the students to get rid of Hamlet. Forget for a moment why he is contemplating self-destruction. Forget the play, character and meaning, and just go to those six words: To be or not to be.

We talked about to and about be and about to be. It means to live, to exist, to breathe, see, think. We talked about or and how it disturbs a sentence. We spent a lot of time on not. That not changes everything. And we talked about what or not does to make the second to be so different from the first.

We talked about what Shakespeare didn't say. He didn't use the most dramatic words he could have. He didn't say To live or not to live, To die or not to die, To live or die—all of which mean the same thing. It would be a lot simpler to say To die or not to die than it is to say To be or not to be. We can easily find images for to live and to die. In comparison, to be is non-threatening, non-violent.

The choice of words, as it turns out, tells us something about Hamlet—who he is, how he thinks. But you don't need to know everything about him at this point. If you can reach into yourself and find a way of making Hamlet's to be have as much force as to live in ordinary speech, you've done all that needs to be done. You have experienced the words.

Of course, if it took three hours to experience every six words, getting the whole speech completed would take forever. But you get better at experiencing words. You won't always have to reduce every word to its most basic meaning. And once you make the words work for you, there is a reward worthy of the effort. You begin to make the words yours—you find you own a small part of Shakespeare's English.

Experiencing Poetry as an Actor

Poetry is a good place to hone your skills, because you work with the words and their meanings without concerning yourself with the character you are portraying or the action of a scene. If there is a character behind the poetry, it is usually that of the poet. If there is an action, it is described, not performed.

Walt Whitman's poetry is personal. He speaks directly to his reader about himself—his likes, dislikes, his interests, his pleasures and pains, his personal experiences. How personal is Whitman? Well, his poems were collected under the title *Songs of Myself.* In one of the great favorites of Whitman admirers, he speaks directly to the idea of the personal in his work.

I celebrate myself, and sing myself,
And what I assume you shall assume,
For every atom belonging to me as good belongs to you.

Joanne: *Does any other famous and respected poem in English contain the word "myself" twice in a single line—and in the first line at that? The line is "self"–centered, but it contains two verbs, "celebrate" and "sing," that don't quite fit with "myself" in ordinary usage, that aren't so personal.*

Read the first line aloud several times. Listen to yourself and others around you read it.

You start with I. Say I as if you were the most important person on earth. Say it as if you were the last person on earth. Say it as if you were talking to someone who can't understand a word you say.

The I sits there, at the top of the poem, looking and sounding exactly like your own personal and everyone else's I. I is easy. We experience it often. It's not until you see "celebrate" and "sing" preceded by the "I" that the poem moves away from you and what you are used to.

You do have images and associations that personalize the two verbs. You celebrate holidays, birthdays, promotions, recognition of your talent. You sing a song, sing in a choir, sing like a bird. You can experience I celebrate and I sing *without much effort, although the ideas don't mean much because they feel incomplete.* I celebrate and sing *what?* Myself?

Myself *changes everything. Whitman isn't talking about celebrations of birthdays or special occasions. He's saying he celebrates himself and he does it whenever he feels like it, perhaps all the time.*

When he says: "I sing myself," he means he is the song, words and music, and the singer.

Now read the first line of the poem out loud again.

I celebrate myself, and sing myself.

If there is a difference between how you read them this time and how you did earlier, then to some extent you have experienced Whitman's words. Now you are reading the poem as if you were Walt Whitman.

And, as with Shakespeare, you own one small piece of these words of Whitman's.

By the way, the third line of his poem rescues it from becoming one of the great ego trips of all time. Here Whitman says: For all the atoms that form me also form you.

He is saying my "I" and "you" are made of the same stuff. We are the same. So when I celebrate myself and sing myself, I am celebrating and singing you. I am singing and celebrating all people, every one. Once you know that this is the message of the poem, your experience of his words will change again.

Experiencing Words on Stage

Let's end this discussion by going back to Hamlet for a moment. He is the Prince of Denmark. His father is dead and his father's brother—Hamlet's uncle—is now king. Even worse, Hamlet's widowed mother married her former brother-in-law soon after her first husband died. And Hamlet has reason to believe that his uncle murdered his brother, Hamlet's father. If this is so, then as a prince and the heir to the throne, Hamlet must take action against his uncle. But he finds himself paralyzed—by conscience and reason—and unable to act decisively.

He's a Prince but also he's a student, a thinker, a young man whose mind is opening up to new ideas. Although his studies have been interrupted by the trouble at home, Hamlet's habits of mind, his reliance on thought, his desire to be rational are still with him, and they are evident in his language from the start of the soliloquy.

Joanne: *The experienced actor who plays Hamlet can't come out on stage and recite "To be or not to be" in a big, ringing voice that fills the theater. He may have experienced the words in preparation for the role, he may be so confident that he can now claim some ownership of Elizabethan English that he wants to belt it all out. But he is Hamlet, these words are Hamlet's, and he must speak as Hamlet.*

In the next line of this soliloquy Hamlet asks himself "Whether 'tis nobler in the mind" to suffer the horrors of life than to put an end to the whole mess by killing himself. "Nobler"—more noble—is a very important word here. Hamlet is a nobleman, born to rule. First the actor must experience the word himself. What is noble? What does it mean to be noble?

The actor must take possession of the word for himself.
Then he has to experience it as Prince Hamlet experi-
ences it. But experiencing it as a prince is not part of this
class. That comes later. It's enough now to experience it
as yourself.

No wonder every great and many not so great actors want
to play Hamlet. If the ability to experience the word is
another measure of an actor's skill, to experience Shakespeare's words as given to Hamlet may be the ultimate
exercise of that skill.

An Aside: Landing the Word

Whether actors are speaking, whispering, shouting or
singing, they have to be sure the words they use achieve
their purpose. The words have to be understood as intended by the person voicing them and by the person or
persons to whom they are addressed. Joanne calls this
"landing" the words.

Joanne: *Landing a word is a little like picking it up, with*
its full meaning attached, and handing it to the person or
persons you are addressing. And making sure they have a
firm grip on the meaning when you let it go and become

silent. We all land words on people we are familiar with all the time—on our parents, on friends, on fellow students. It is easy and natural to do so because this is the best way of making sure we will be understood. On stage, using someone else's language, speaking as a character to other characters in a play and including an audience among those on whom you want the words to land is a much different matter. You can't shout every word. You won't always be the only person speaking or the main person in the scene. But what you say is important. It must be heard and understood.

Joanne's emphasis on landing words is particularly useful when you encounter old-fashioned language, dated sentence structure, writing that is organized into lines of an established length, sometimes rhymed lines, with words arranged according to a meter so that there are a fixed number of accented and unaccented syllables per line. It sometimes seems more than enough just to repeat the words in order and make them seem meaningful, while honoring in some way the formal, poetic conventions imposed by the author.

But it is much more complicated than that.

Joanne: *In Shakespeare's* Julius Caesar, *Mark Antony says to the assembled "Friends, Romans, Countrymen" that he has "come to bury Caesar, not to praise him." In fact, he does praise Caesar and desires to turn those friends, Romans, and countrymen against Brutus and the others who killed the emperor. The actor playing Mark Antony has to land his words and his hidden meaning on every person in that immense crowd—as well as on every person in his audience. The actor playing Hamlet, speaking his soliloquy, seems to be landing his words on himself alone, but he also has to land them on every person in his audience.*

Just as landing an aircraft at its assigned destination is necessary for a flight to be completed successfully, so the actor must land the playwright's words and meanings on the other actors and the members of the audience for the play to achieve its purpose and full effect. And the job of landing varies from play to play and character to character. To land his message, Mark Antony uses up the full runway. In contrast, Hamlet lands his message on a dime.

So landing is not a simple matter. Almost nothing in great acting is. (Great acting can make the impossibly difficult look easy, but don't let brilliance fool you.) Each of Joanne's seven steps will help you discover how to land the message you bring, how to identify who you are bringing the message to, and how to understand what your message must convey to those who receive it.

From that point on, it's up to you.

THE SEVEN STEPS

A Summary

How a Prop Saved My Life: A True Story

A Summary

The order in which the steps are presented in this introduction is not entirely arbitrary. It begins with the two steps that must be grasped by the student in order to master the others. *Inner Life* and *Focus* ask you to recognize and make use of the very human, very common practice of moving between the real, immediate outer life surrounding us now—where people work and food is grown and we floss our teeth before bed—and the inner life—which is imagined, remembered, borrowed, begged, pilfered and invented. In the inner life anything can happen, but nothing much usually does–except when inner and outer become confused in a character's mind, which happens often in drama.

Climbing these seven steps lifts you above the level where you started and makes it easier to begin viewing your surroundings as an actor. That's when your surroundings change and expand. Climbing those same steps over and over, as you work on your performance, strengthens you and gives you reason to feel more confident of yourself. And they can do more:

How a Prop Saved My Life: A True Story

Joanne: *We were doing* Long Day's Journey into Night. *And I was playing Mary Tyrone, the mother, the wife, the addict, who has an immense presence in that play—she reaches into every nook and cranny. It was a huge role, and I was co-directing. I was tired. At curtain opening night my husband, James Tyrone, a well-known actor, and I came on stage right after breakfast.*

When we walked out, I had an outer life experience of the worst possible kind for an actor. I found I was not Mary Tyrone, not in Mary Tyrone's home, not even in the neighborhood. I saw a friend and fellow actor next to me wearing a very unbecoming costume. I knew he wore shabby clothes because he was playing the part of my famous actor husband James Tyrone, who was a cheapskate. But I forgot that he was my husband and a cheapskate when I saw, beyond him, the audience, a sloping wall of faces.

I panicked. I was lost on stage, empty of ideas, and destitute. And then I saw a prop, a coffee pot on the table. And I saw it not as Joanne Linville but as Mary Tyrone. The coffee pot was from my inner life. It was Mary's shining silver coffee pot. It was as if the pot had come out of the play and found me. I went over and clasped that pot between my hands. Mary would do that, to find out if the coffee was hot. The prop itself was cold, but I remembered what warm coffee pots feel like and suddenly my hands were warm. I took my time pouring coffee, adding cream and sugar, stirring, placing the wet spoon where it could not stain my tablecloth.

Finally I was able to look up and see James Tyrone, my husband of thirty-odd years, my great love and nemesis, who with my sons was entwined around me, clinging to me like those climbing vines that strangle the trees that support them. As Mary I was an addict trying to break a dependency on morphine, a legal and available drug at the time. I was always on the verge of backsliding. In Eugene O'Neill's stage directions Mary's hands are always moving, and I was using that. I couldn't keep my hands still and didn't want others to notice them.

Seeing that coffee pot gave me, as the lost Joanne Linville, a real thing from the play, and it saved me. It pulled me back into the place. What was even better, the coffee pot gave Mary something real to do with her uncontrollable hands—touch the pot, pour the coffee, stir the cream.

This is a true story, and it's a good example of how the steps are used to strengthen a performance. Mary's inner life fills her with thoughts of her drug addiction, of her sick son, of her husband who won't spend money on proper medical care. In her outer life she focuses on her home, on the man who is her husband, on the coffee pot that will give her something to do with her hands. She has to be in her present tense to walk with him and to pour the coffee, but the past, the disillusionment and the drugs and a terrible tragedy—the death of a child years before—pull at her like a riptide.

Her breathing changes when she sees the pot as something solid for her to cling to.

Experiencing the word and experiencing tenses aren't directly involved in this opening moment of the play. But Mary is experiencing physical and mental torment that will influence how she uses the words she is given to say. The drugs, the constant quarrels, her younger son's illness, her husband's cheapness, her older son's utter failure and the alcohol all the men consume—all this shapes her words. Her mind and her words move from past to present to future and back, and almost everywhere her attention stops, she finds unhappiness.

There are, I am pleased to say, a few welcome exceptions to Mary's misery. When she has reason to laugh and enjoy herself, as she does occasionally, an Irish lilt returns to her voice, coming from her past, from a happier, more carefree youth—as a convent student. A convent girl's life isn't always thought of as carefree, but compared to her home life, with James Tyrone and the sons always bickering and boozing, her past as an innocent young girl is a source of faded joy to her. What fun it was as an actress to add that lilt to Mary's speech. And what a relief.

ABOUT THE AUTHORS

Joanne Linville

In Joanne Linville's best known, if not her favorite, role as an actress, she appeared in *Star Trek: The Original Series* playing the Romulan Commander. She was the first female Romulan featured in an episode, and the only female character to ignite a spark of romance in the otherwise emotionless Dr. Spock. It remains a memorable episode from the series.

Her professional career began when television was young and drama was broadcast live. For the actor, that meant doing it right the first time because there would only be that first time. She appeared in shows that are associated with quality programming of the early decades: *Alfred Hitchcock Presents, Studio One, Kraft Television Theater, DuPont Show of the Week, Twilight Zone, Gunsmoke, Ben Casey, Streets of San Francisco, The FBI, Hawaii 5-0, Dynasty,* and *L. A. Law.*

Her movie credits include *The Goddess, Scorpio, A Star is Born, Gable and Lombard, The Seduction.* More recently she appeared in *The James Dean Story,* directed by her former husband, Mark Rydell. She and Mark are the parents of two children, Christopher and Amy.

Foremost among the people who influenced Joanne's acting career and her early work as a teacher was Stella Adler, with whom she studied when she moved to New York City. Born into a theatrical family, the daughter of Jacob B. Adler, a great tragedian of the Yiddish Theater, Stella had her stage debut at age four. As a young woman she acted in Europe and South America as well as in the United States. She studied at N.Y.U. and took classes with many of the most important actor/teachers of the period, including Konstantin Stanislavsky, whose influence on acting and theatrical vision is as powerful today as it was almost a century ago. Stella was a member of the Group Theatre, perhaps the most respected and influential acting ensemble in the American theater of the last century. She appeared in several films.

She founded the Stella Adler Conservatory in 1949. Among her students were Marlon Brando, Robert De Niro and Warren Beatty. Joanne studied with her and later was one of the founders the Stella Adler Conservatory which opened in Hollywood, California, in 1985.

She was also inspired by the work of Angna Enters, one of the most gifted non-speaking actors of all time. Enters' innovations were so unique that critics gave her work a name, dance/mime—which Enters did not think appropriate. She toured as a one-person program for many years. Her indescribable performances remain vividly alive in the memories of those fortunate enough to

Film stills, top to bottom:

As the Romulan Commander on Star Trek: The Original Series

With Lloyd Bridges in a Studio One Production

Bottom two stills:

Twilight Zone episode "The Passerby"

have seen her on her stage. She developed the programs, designed and made her costumes and designed her sets. She was also a painter and writer. She was not comfortable in the role of teacher, but those who studied with her said that she had a major influence on their work. For a brief period Enters was associated with the Stella Adler Conservatory.

Joanne says she has learned more about acting from her students than from the formal teaching she received. But her love for, and commitment to, the craft of acting began when she started studying with Stella Adler, and she strives through her teaching to ensure that Stella's inspiration continues to reach and influence new generations of actors.

John Deck

A Santa Cruz-based writer, John Deck has published a novel, a collection of short stories and a non-fiction book about retirement living in mobile home communities. He has written plays and screenplays and has taught writing, worked in computer documentation, written advertising copy and contributed to educational texts.

He has known Joanne Linville all his life, has followed her career closely from its beginning and has discussed the arts—including acting, the theater and film—with her extensively over many years.

In working on this book, Deck discussed Joanne's seven steps at great length with her as they evolved through her teaching. He attended her acting classes and spoke with students and former students.

He also used tapes recorded by Joe D'Agosto, one of Joanne's former students, who worked tirelessly recording, and also transcribing, several classes.

Both authors wish to thank Joe D'Agosto for his selfless and devoted contribution to this publication.

pp 124 -127: *Joanne Linville and students during a typical acting workshop at the Stella Adler West*

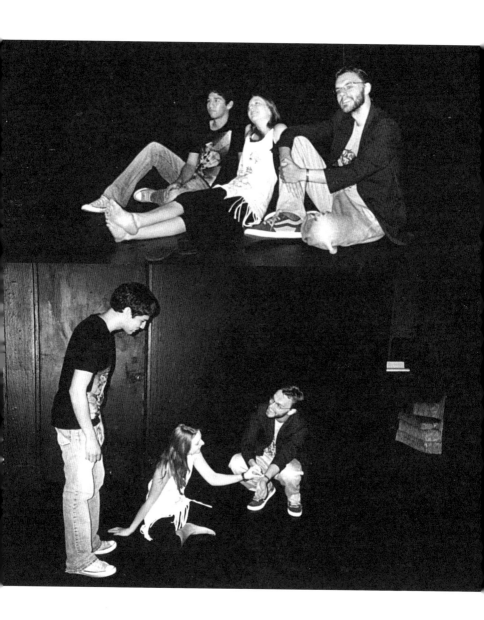